the CHROME CHAIR

the CHROME CHAIR

DANIELLE DEVEREAUX

Riddle Fence Debuts
St. John's, NL

THE CHROME CHAIR
Copyright © 2024 by Danielle Devereaux

Riddle Fence Publishing Inc.
PO Box 7092
St. John's, NL A1E 3Y3, Canada
www.riddlefence.com

The publisher gratefully acknowledges the support of the Canada Council for the Arts, the Newfoundland and Labrador Arts Council, and the Government of NL.

Riddle Fence Publishing acknowledges the land on which we work as the ancestral homelands of the Beothuk, whose culture has now been erased forever. We also acknowledge the island of Ktaqmkuk (Newfoundland) as the unceded, traditional territory of the Beothuk and the Mi'kmaq. And we acknowledge Labrador as the traditional and ancestral homelands of the Innu of Nitassinan, the Inuit of Nunatsiavut, and the Inuit of NunatuKavut.

Cover and text design by: Graham Blair
Cover art by: Stacey Croucher
Edited by: Sandra Ridley

Printed and bound in Canada

Library and Archives Canada Cataloguing in Publication
Title: The chrome chair / Danielle Devereaux.
Names: Devereaux, Danielle, author.
Description: Poems.
Identifiers: Canadiana (print) 20230590454 | Canadiana (ebook) 20230590489 | ISBN 9781738151509 (softcover) | ISBN 9781738151516 (EPUB)
Subjects: LCGFT: Poetry.
Classification: LCC PS8607.E94 C57 2024 | DDC C811/.6—dc23

We were promised a seat at the table of nations;
what we got was a chrome chair.

—NEWFOUNDLAND AND LABRADOR
HISTORICAL SOCIETY SYMPOSIUM, 2003

Contents

Splinter

splinter, n. 1. A rough (usually long, thin, and sharp-edged) piece of wood, bone, stone, etc., split or broken off, esp. as the result of violent impact; a chip, fragment, or shiver. 2. Used (chiefly with negatives) to denote a very small piece or amount, or something of little or no value, e.g.: She is not worth the splinter of a spear.

splinter, v. 1. transitive. To break or split into splinters or long narrow pieces, or in such a way as to leave a rough jagged end or projections. 2. intransitive. To split; to break, burst, or fly into fragments; to come away in splinters.

The Chrome Chair

We were promised a seat at the table of nations;
what we got was a chrome chair.

—On Newfoundland's confederation with
Canada, Newfoundland and Labrador
Historical Society Symposium, 2003

Chrome chairs are all the rage on Queen Street
in Toronto. Redone in soft, faux leather
petroleum product. Shade: bone china.
A make-work colour for the salt-of-the-earth
maid. Sleek chrome legs shined up like

Christmas tinsel. The chrome table in my
kitchen would fetch a pretty penny. Nan
must've liked this table, the glamour
of its lipstick-red top, shapely silver legs.
She didn't keep much no longer of use, or

out of fashion, but my table stayed. Stored
in a shed by the sea. The matching chairs have
disappeared, but the wipe-clean Arborite is
smooth, nick-free. The chrome band of its edge
gleams like the bumper of a brand-new car, wet

capelin. Can you hear them? The kids
from Queen Street? Revving up their SUVs for a trip
Down East. Crossing the ocean in search of authentic
chrome. Tables leaning on drafty walls, chairs
stacked behind idle fishing gear and dusty doll's clothes.

The old ladies will say,
Go on, take 'em, what odds.
I've got a new set from Kent's.

Glint of chrome legs
cuts through the fog.

Sculpin

A photo of me as a kid at the beach
clutching capelin like medals on ribbons.
Another of me on the wharf, dangling
a sculpin, catgut

hooked in his throat. My great uncle
squinting beside me, pipe hooked over his lip.
"He's no good, maid, ugly as sin. Here,
I throws him back." Snap.

O hideous sculpin,
Caliban of the sea,
your mother was the devil
and your father ate whore's eggs.

A yearbook photo of my high school
swim team, me shining, happy and wet
from the pool. We graduate and there is
no cod. Boats on the beach, lost

culture. I wonder how this affects
me: townie-teen who hooked a
sculpin one summer, visiting
nan and pop around the bay.

O throat-scarred sculpin,
do you remember me?
My mother grew up on Patrick Street
and my father gets seasick.

Down the street the price of fish
at Ches's has gone up
drastically.

I don't let on,
but I only ever ordered
chips and gravy.

Bury Me in Newfoundland

Don't bother with a box. Lay me
right in the rock, naked. Put a marker

if you must. On a piece of driftwood,
burn my name but know

I won't be here long. Last fistful of dirt
and I'm gone. Bone splinters, shedding skin,

shards of me marble the dark grey granite. I am
jagged cliff edge. Spools of hair tumble, reach down

along the sharp, red sand, under the smooth
backs of beach rocks. I am seaweed,

licking salt from the waves. My teeth shatter
on the shelved slate below, washed in white foam,

rubbed with salt. I am broken seashells,
scraping and pulling in time with the tide.

My heart finds a barren,
caresses the carpet of moss

'til blood seeps through—partridgeberry,
the rich, red sting.

Good Luck

These houses have been repainted—peach,
pale blue, light green—the laundry hasn't
changed. Sport socks twist, tangle in the line,
faded blue jeans press forward, too heavy

to flip in the wind, still damp when the sun
goes down. That night, when the man and
woman started screaming, the girl
took her little brother next door. The neighbour

smiled, gave them milky tea and toast,
homemade bread with Good Luck
margarine. The radio played loud. They slept
on the pullout couch. This was usual.

It would be okay. In the morning
the girl covered her mother's bare legs
with the throw from Pipers—squares of
hearts and houses—and called 911.

She pulled the pink tank top back down over
her mother's belly, tried not to step in the blood.
Later, she felt glad that she'd left her little brother
next door, eating Arrowroots, watching cartoons.

Goodwill

1.

You're colouring at the kitchen table when the radio
says they've located Dana Bradley. A man and a boy
looking for a Christmas tree found a dead girl. Foul play
is suspected. "Jesus." Your mother stops sweeping.

She sits beside you. "Jesus Christ." Her fingers grip
the top of your skinny arm. "Promise me, promise
you'll never, ever, hitchhike. Promise you'll never
go anywhere with a stranger." You cross your heart,

but you're five and cannot imagine going anywhere
without your mother. She opens a bottle of Cutex,
scrubs the chipped, red polish off your fingernails
and will never repaint them. Disappears upstairs,

finds your favourite bathing suit, the turquoise blue
bikini, stuffs it in the green garbage bag marked
Goodwill. You keep your word. Even when you're 12,
it's raining, you've spent your bus money on onion rings

at the mall, you do not stick out your thumb.
And when the car stops anyway, you keep walking,
feel her fingers gripping the top of your skinny arm.
No. You do not want a ride.

2.

The newspapers keep running yearbook photos of
Kristen French and Leslie Mahaffy. You're also
15. You cannot connect their smiles to ditches,
body parts in concrete. You wonder after Mrs. Lam,

the Chinese woman next door. She doesn't speak
or read English. Perhaps these are photos of two
girls who've won medals, capsized and survived,
girls who will cut their own faces from the papers,

paste them in scrapbooks. You read that Kristen French
said some things are worth dying for, an echo
from your little book of Christian saints. Saint Maria
Goretti, the little girl who loved God and hated sin,

said the same thing. Died too, because someone else
wanted her body. You're tired of understanding
English. It's Saturday, your father folds the newspaper
twice, drops it in the trash, gets in the car. Comes home

from Canadian Tire with a personal safety alarm.
Loop the rope around your wrist, in an emergency,
pull: scream like a siren. "You can put it in your purse."
Now you will have to buy a purse. He begins to jog

with you, is pleased when you sprint past him.
He is a fit man. If you can outrun your father,
perhaps you can outrun men who do not love you.
Men who will look at your running shorts and thighs,
think: *switchblade*.

3.

You move away for work. Your mother
sends an email, subject heading: *Staying
Safe: Wisdom for Women.* Tips include
what to do if someone throws you

into the trunk of your own car. You don't
own a fucking car. You are a 27-year-old
feminist. You walk home alone in the dark.
Fast. On well-lit streets, wearing good running

shoes, stroking the plastic shell of your
personal safety alarm. Don't delete the email.
You're homesick. You find a bike trail. Tall trees
console you. You smile at boys on bikes. Later,

you call your mother, tell her your discovery,
tell her it was a beautiful, sunny day.
Your mother is watching the evening news.
She says police have just found the naked body

of a woman on a cycling path. Ardeth Wood,
age 27, was biking in broad daylight. "You
won't go on that trail alone again, will you?"
You thought you'd outgrow this. "Promise me."

Skincare Aisle, Shoppers Drug Mart

I've been standing in skincare for twenty minutes,
(dermobiotic wrinkle reducer, Revitalift, Rejuveness,
Oil of Olay), when the woman behind the counter asks
if she can help. I rub my forehead, feel fine lines,
"Just looking, thanks." She smiles. Something—the dip
of her upper lip, the fluorescents, the way the letters

shine on the packaging—makes me think of Renee.
A girl I knew from high school, basketball, soccer.
I smile back. Did Renee have a sister?
I don't remember a sister—it was years ago,
we were teenagers, and there were so many girls
at the wake. Wet eyes, splotchy faces, the hum
of too many drugstore perfumes.

There'd been a photo in *The Telegram*: car
buckled like a Coke tin against a telephone pole.

I remember laying a sympathy card
in the cardholder, standing by the casket,
trying to pray. The pink satin lining of the open
coffin, blonde highlights in her brown hair.

The photo from the newspaper,
the car, the pole,
her pretty face undamaged.

Two-storey, Semi-detached

There's been a death in the house.
My house, mirror of the one in mourning,
knows. Joined at the kitchen,
stairway, bathroom, separated by wall-
paper, Gyproc, wood. This is not enough
to keep out the smell of baked bread,
Sunday dinner, grief. Sudden death.
Like a shock of skull against
the cupboard door left open.
I touch wood—door frames, banisters.
Cringe at the creak of loose floorboards.
Even this living room
is full of loss.

Home Renos

Interlocking laminate?
Cushion floor?
Ceramic tile?
Hardwood?

    No.
What I want is the canvas from my mother's
old kitchen. Stamped squares. A mosaic of brown,
cream, and orange. Spanish tiles for a Newfoundland

kitchen. Earth tones to match the harvest-gold fridge
and stove, wrist of a Portuguese sailor considering
a watch down to Woolworth's. My mother loved that
floor because it didn't show the dirt. I understand

now that this was like magic—flaky bits of onion
skin and spattered chili could wait 'til Saturday,
and if Saturday was sunny, 'til sometime else.
It would last forever, and she didn't flinch when we

stomped in wearing soccer cleats, dropped heavy-
bottomed pots. But I think she chose it because she
went to Spain once, before marriage and me. Smiled
at Spanish fellas who thought she looked exotic.

When Dad hauled that floor up it was still in good
shape, and would've done, if she knew someone with
her exact kitchen measurements, but she didn't.
So it went to the dump. Think it still hides the dirt?

City Planning, St. John's

In honour of Sobeys, Merrymeeting Rd.

If I wanted to live like a mouse, trapped
in a dresser drawer, I'd move to Mississauga.
In Mississauga, I wouldn't worry about the vinyl
siding of small cities, grocery stores eating green fields.

I wouldn't stand petitioning on pressure-treated
porches to hear: *it'll be so convenient; well dear,*
that's progress when I talk of rezoning, Sobeys
on a soccer pitch, and fat children. In Mississauga,

I'd take the elevator to my very own shelf.
Curl up in my IKEA corner. Count my
nine-to-five findings. Celebrate the success
of another snapped-neck-free day.

Mainland Man

I want a mainland man.
Accent like a three-piece
suit, Rolex wristwatch,
cowboy boots.

I want a mainland man.
A voice on ice, slick with
Alberta oil. Toronto,
Ottawa, Montreal.

And oh, that mainland man wants
Newfoundland alright. Salty as cod tongues,
fish and brewis, homemade bread with
sex and tea in the woods.

Sweet handsome, dansome mainland man,
you've no time for a townie girl
with the salt schooled from her throat,
but my bloodline runs rogue

bayman, sir,
and I boils a mean kettle.

Cardiogram

Since you left, I've had a bad heart,
always whinging and moaning
for attention. *Watch me! Lookit, watch!*
Cartwheels and backflips 'til she

smacks into the corner of the coffee table.
I yell at her to give it a rest. She just sits there,
shaking. Builds pillow forts while we
watch TV, promises to be more *careful*,

but by 10 p.m. she's bored and overtired, refuses
to go to bed. I have to chase her up the stairs.
The two of us slip-sliding around
on the linoleum. My heart knows she's been bad,

plasters the fridge with homemade cards, a bloody
red blot of herself pressed to pink construction paper:
I ♥ you. But she's a fickle little bugger, this one,
and we both know it's not true.

Crush

It's not you, it's me.
You're a cool cat
with a sandpaper purr,

it's my heart
racing. Pet mouse
on a wire wheel.

One stray touch
of your silk paw
spins me.

Leave the room,
my heart'll curl up
in her corner.

Throb.

Diet Tips

Worry pooled in the gut is highly
effective, a backwash of gravel
and sand. Words said and not said

matted with strands of hair. I eat
nothing but Saltines and club soda.
Wake doubled over, cough up

splintered glass. My stomach has
caved in on itself and caught fire,
but damn do I look hot in blue jeans.

La Cache Close-out Sale, Queen Street

This is the sweater I bought the day you
put your hand on my thigh. Your hand
on my thigh meant: maybe. If you weren't
driving home to someone else.

$119 marked down to 15—a steal.
All sales final. The saleslady
cut the tags so I could wear it home.
It was cold. I was wearing a thin shirt.

It's summer now. I've no call to wear this
sweater, no reason to think of your hand
on my thigh. Not that I regret it. It's a nice
sweater. It was a good buy.

Quelle Affaire

"You are what you eat," dieters are told.
I ate my lover's wedding band; now I'm good as gold.

Conservation Policies

I hoard hurt the way a squirrel stores nuts.
See where the side of my face swells?
My gums are raw as guts. I check my stash

frequently. The counting calms me.
All those hurts lined up like air cadets
or almonds: look what you did, what you

made me do. You'll know me when I'm
an old woman. I'll be the one with ratty
fingernails. Jowls.

Wedding Cake

Three-tiered and tremendous, sugar roses
red enough to make chipped rental china
great again. There are no cupcakes here;

this bakery is not artisanal and the bride and groom
are tired. She smiles on, intent on her task. He looks
forlorn, standing straight beside his brittle bride, eyes

fixed on the wide window of the bar across the way.
The bartender is broad-shouldered and beautiful.
Pulling beer, slicing limes, he grins and is tipped

handsomely. Even if our sad groom could close
his painted eyes, he'd still see that smile, ache
for a taste of those cheekbones—just a tiny slice.

I've Got a Cake

With your name on it, or I would, if this kitchen
weren't such a disaster, or I owned a bakery. There's an idea!
My own little shop—display cases and a cash

register. Row upon row of (lemon, vanilla, chocolate)
cake, with your name on it. Except, the customers,
they'd be wanting their own names on cake, change

for the parking meter. And the frosting, always
fussier than I think it'll be, the right sweet
consistency, all those goddamn crumbs.

Newfoundland Spring

Here is my heart as a hollow thing:
a pink plastic egg, a ceramic gnome,
a real milk chocolate, anthropomorphic
ladybug holding a tulip.

My children love these hollow objects.

They love to squeeze them
in their squishy fists,
hug them to their own miraculous
beating hearts.

And when the ladybug, still in her cellophane-
windowed cardboard box, takes a knock, hits
the tiled kitchen floor, splinters, they are sad.
For a heartbeat. Then tear open the pretty
paper box, gobble up the broken pieces.

Insomniac

My fool heart is happy enough
loving on the world in the front-step
sun. How beautiful shines the world
in the front-step sun! Dandelions sneak
up where the sidewalk splits—such bright
yellow pluck! And the shattered glass

near the curb glimmers. But we can't
sit here forever. She flinches, my heart,
cracking open the heavy front door. I sigh.
The state of this house/the state of the world:
maggoty with stuff and an empty fridge,
sink scum, and stacks of recycling.

Under the duvet, my heart can't remember
the sun. *Da-dump*, *da-dump*ing
her worries: the dandelion, despite its pluck,
will never be enough to save the bees;
the glittering glass, a trap to slash
some tender paw, a child's bare knee.

If it's clear skies tomorrow, I'll cut her loose.
A few choice nicks with my best
steak knife—slice, slip. Set her free
to follow the sun. I hope by nightfall
she's near a flower bed, lays down for a rest.
It'll sting a bit, sure, but I might get some sleep.

Incognito

Well-executed I'm undetectable or maybe
outlandish, a blue marzipan
bouffant.
Poorly done I'm dead squirrel,
synthetic rug. Height of high seven-
teenth century fashion. These days,
queen of the ill.

Playthings

Spend too much time playing, dreaming your
little girl dreams with hair clips, fake
lipstick, mirror mirror, the right pink glitter
wand, and bam! Your legs will turn so thin,

so long, they'll barely support the weight
of your new breasts,
but never mind. Think of the shoes:
open-toed peach stilettos, sweet

little white pumps with pink at the heel and toe.
The Peaches 'n Cream ball gown, the Day-to-Night
hot-pink business suit, and your fave, the prom queen,
pretty-in-pink-hand-over-the-tiara dream dress.

So what if your mother's a German
porn doll, you're better than her.
You have careers; fasten that faux-
metal stethoscope around your neck

and stand proud: proof
that accessories, ladies,
are what we make of them.
Slip that tapered lab coat

over your mini-skirt, sparkling white from top
to toe like a tanned Malibu angel, and know,
thanks to you, girls all over the world set their
sights on medical science. *But girls*, you say,

for God's sake girls. Let's do it with a titchy bit of
glamour. Feminists might say you're a bad influence,
but they're not your problem. Your problem
is Ken. G.I. Joe was right, Ken is gay—

the sculpted hair, the shining smile, those pecs.
You're gutted. Cinderella and Prince Charming,
Snow White and that other Prince Charming,
Beauty and the Beast, Ken and you—the blonde

hair, the big boobs, the hot pink box. Ruined.
And about those shoes, they never did fit,
not even the sweet little white pumps with pink
at the heel and toe, and though you haven't eaten

anything since, well, ever, your favourite skirt
(the reversible one—
a sensible pink cotton blend by day, sexy
fuchsia chiffon by night), the skirt that slays

your Day-to-Night Barbie business suit
pops open whenever you sit.
Your pink corvette overturned in a ditch, and you
naked from the waist down, still smiling.

Double Dactyl

Inkkity-pinkkity
Virginia Woolf
Said a gal needs a
Room of her own.

Critics complained she was
Feminist-radical.
She closed up her door and
They left her alone.

Feminists in Heaven

Does the word "Persons" in section 24 of the British North America Act
1867 include female persons? . . . The question is answered in the negative.

—Supreme Court of Canada, 1928

To hell with the Rosary, Emily Murphy arrived
prepared to give God a piece of her mind. Heaven

help the policymaker to argue He could not hold court
with a woman. Adam and Eve in the Garden! The Book

needs a rewrite. She would start a petition. Turns out policy-
makers go to purgatory, and God never did come back from

the Azores. Not much for the Famous Five to do here but form
a curling team—hurry, hurry hard to glory. There's a rink to beat
at the Brier.

Academic Articles: "The Cartesian Masculinization of Thought" (S. Bordo, 1986)

Similar to shooting at a conveyor-belt parade of sitting ducks at the town fair, here we take aim at cardboard cutouts of the bust of René Descartes (moustached, sporting the high, ruffled collar of a French aristocrat). A proponent of vivisection, Descartes claimed animals are not self-aware, and therefore do not feel pain. Knock the block off three mini-Descartes, and a siren will scream, a neon sign on the back wall will scroll and flash: *I think therefore I am. I think therefore I am. I think.* And you'll win a prize: a signed copy of the seminal ecofeminist text *The Death of Nature.* What a lucky duck.

We ♥ the Animals

When the television work dried up and Jerry the Man died, Travis the Chimp grew forlorn. And also bored. With no Jerry, there were no joyrides in the company tow truck or family 4Runner, no trips to the ice cream parlour. There was just Sandy the Woman, who'd paid the $50K to own him, crying on the couch, *Travis, come comb mommy's hair.* She'd come home from T.J. Maxx with bags full of trinkets for the trinket shelves, high-heeled shoes, and chimp-sized sweaters.

Wild chimpanzees eat termites and berries, the occasional monkey. They have a lot of sex. On Rock Rimmon Road in Stamford, Connecticut, Travis had three TVs and a computer. He drank Tropicana orange juice and ate Lindt chocolates. It was fine. Until the day he ripped a woman apart. One hand and the other arm, next her entire face. The newspapers hypothesized the chimp had escaped to try to go for a ride; the woman had only come by to help Sandy coax him back inside.

Sandy did try to stop her chimp-child. Hit him with a shovel, stabbed him with a kitchen knife three times in the back. On the *Today Show*, she said Travis turned toward her then. She could see the hurt in his eyes, what he was thinking: "He looked at me, like, 'Mom, why'd you do that?'" The show host nods sympathetically. Sympathy looks good on TV. Besides, he's never looked into the eyes of a dying chimpanzee. If he had, he might've seen something a little different, something a little more like this: *You goddamn bloody humans, you goddamn bloody bitch.*

Queen

After Sylvia Plath

I am a riddle nine times over.
Egyptian queen, waiting. The witch's
black shadow, a spilt tumbler of salt.
Electricity, bright lights on legs.
Sunday afternoons wrapped in heavy
duvets. The spinster's sleek companion.
Adored: a diva in glorious
furs. Abandoned: they drown my children;
say I'm the one who steals baby's breath.

Her Mother's Daughter

After Angela Ball

To have red lipstick for a mother
is to pray for straight teeth.

To have a rice cake for a mother means
pouring skim milk over Special K.

To have a curling iron for a mother
is to long for blonde hair.

To have a street light for a mother
is to travel only in pairs.

To have a bible for a mother means
impeccable posture.

If your mother is a blue flame, you suck
ice cubes. Leave candles unattended.

My mother is a Sunday dress. I own
a springform pan, keep boxes
of graham crackers on hand.

My mother is a garden party. I shop
at white elephant tables, drink
tea from chipped china.

My mother is a carnival. I grow
a beard, try my luck with the
strong man.

Spinster

spinster, n. [f. SPIN v. + -STER.] 1. A woman *still unmarried* and considered unlikely ever to do so; esp. one who has remained single beyond the typical age for marriage, *an old maid*. 2. A person (esp. a woman or girl) who spins wool, flax, cotton, or another textile fibre into thread or yarn, esp. *one who practises spinning as a regular occupation*.

yarn, n. 1. Spun fibre, as of cotton, silk, wool, flax, etc. 2. To spin a yarn (figurative, originally nautical slang), to tell a story (usually a long one); also, 'to pitch a tale'. Hence yarn = a (long) story or tale: sometimes implying one of a marvellous or incredible kind; also, a mere tale.

How to Be a Spinster, Circa 2010

Eating alone in restaurants is
discouraged. If you must, bring
notepads, a good book.

One glass of wine with dinner.
White. Do not order cappuccino.
Froth makes you look

available. You're not. Acquire
a taste for chamomile, Earl Grey.
True, your tongue may want

to slide along the smooth, hard
edge of a belt buckle.
Perhaps you could swallow

all the buttons down the front
of a plaid shirt. Boil water.
See: acquired tastes.

Rachel Carson Writes to Her Father

. . . an affectionate but almost irrelevant parent.

—Linda Lear, *Rachel Carson: Witness for Nature*

When Mother agreed to marry you,
she must've imagined your dancing blue
eyes would be enough. By the time

I was born, she could no longer bear
to look into them. In my memory you just
sit in corners, smiling. I want to draw the dance
in your eyes, out your mouth: Speak, Papa, talk

me a blue streak. Do you remember my first book?
I drew animals for you: a mouse, a fish, a frog,
an owl, a bunny, a dog, a hen, and a canary.
You kissed the top of my head, said *how*

nice. Imagine, Papa, if you'd gotten up
from your chair, come with me to the front yard
to search for my animal friends. We look
in the grass for a frog, turn our heads and find

an elephant wearing a tasseled headdress.
A travelling circus. You take my hand, run
to the road. A man, glamorous in a gold turban,
lifts me onto the elephant. I learn to do handstands

on its great, grey back, dazzle crowds with
my sparkling tiara. You take to the trapeze,
dance through the air in blue sequins.

Mrs. Carson Writes to
Her Daughter, Rachel

The best thing to do with want is
swallow it. Quick and whole—

a shucked oyster. This is no time for your fine
scientific mind. Your logbooks and labels.

Put your pencil back in its place. Once
I tried to sketch want. First, it looked like

nothing—a jagged old can, a high-heeled
shoe. Then, a page of eyes blinking grey-black

lead. They looked like silverfish. Swallow it,
love, quick and whole. A shucked oyster.

Rachel Carson Writes to Her Sister

Perhaps you're right, Mother did love me best.
But she did love you, Marian. Don't you remember
her smile when you brought home those school readers

she so adored? Their drawings and little lessons
for the out-of-doors—
she couldn't wait for your backyard excursions.

Only our brother kicked at moss and bark, and
when she turned her head, threw rocks at birds
she'd pointed to and named. And you whined,

Marian, always thirsty or hungry, longing instead
to go inside, play jacks with the girls who lived in town
and wore store-bought dresses. Remember that summer,

when I was five and you fifteen? Those girls, they
envied you then, their ruffles and bows no match for a face
like fine china. After school you walked to town, smiled

at men who even then
looked at the plush red-pink of your lips
and thought: ribbons, silk stockings, *bourbon.*

Rachel Carson Writes to Her College Mentor, Mary Scott Skinker

It's true you changed my life, turned me on
to science. Because of you, I studied the sea.
My biographers say it was your passion

for teaching, your conviction that hard
science does so suit young women. You
must've known it was also the way you wore

red lipstick, a gown each night to dinner. Glamorous
as a starfish. Saturday evenings a fresh flower pinned
at your waist, a gift from the German suitor you left

for a PhD. How I longed to bring wildflower bouquets
to your small study, sit beside you, pore through books
on botany: *This, Miss Skinker, is foxglove beard tongue.*

You would look into my eyes, smile: *Why yes,
so it is. Now Rachel, do stop biting your lip.*

But Miss Skinker, if I did, how would I keep
from kissing yours?

Career Trajectory: Miss Mary Scott Skinker, PhD

At Pennsylvania College for Women, Mary Scott Skinker was science. Grace and high standards. Students admired Miss Skinker, wanted to be science too. Miss Coolidge, college president, thought science an inappropriate discipline for women. Miss Skinker left. She found a job at the Bureau of Animal Industry, US Department of Agriculture, Zoological Division. She earned a PhD. Dr. Mary Scott Skinker worked under the direction of Dr. Eloise B. Cram, scientist. Her team worked primarily in helminthology, the study of parasitic worms. Mostly, they studied the parasites of poultry, enjoyed breakthrough results. They were an unusual group, unmarried, and women. When Dr. Cram left for the Hygienic Laboratory, US Public Health Service, Miss Skinker did not. She had no seniority, having spent too much time teaching science at the Pennsylvania College for Women. The new supervising parasitologist thought science an inappropriate discipline for women. When he spoke to Dr. Mary Scott Skinker he liked to tease, to call her an old maid, spinster. At the Bureau of Animal Industry, US Department of Agriculture, Zoological Division, Mary Scott Skinker was not science. Grace and high standards. Eventually, she returned to teaching. Another college for women. Feminists suggest this situation was not unusual. Still, she hadn't seen it coming. Through her microscope, science always seemed so close.

They Loved These Things Too
After Lisa Jarnot

The sun the moon the stars and the telescopes the microscopes
the periodic table the pulp the paper the ice cubes and the
chesterfields the baseball fields the bungalows in rows and
coming home but mostly going and the washing machines
and melamine and also certain quiz shows and Tupperware
in different shapes and aluminum they loved the herbicides
the fungicides insecticides and cranberries Thanksgiving and
baked Alaskas these they loved as if they loved the wives who
baked them they loved the roadside motels and the automobiles
and the way the waitresses asked them what they wanted
and then they loved the choice of pies to choose *and the sea
they loved the sea* or at least the seaside views and the smell of
coconut they loved sunglasses and the blue of swimming pools
and also they loved all things shaped like rocket launchers and
they loved the zoo.

How to Clean Everything: C

One must not underestimate the utility of a clear conscience. Benefit number one: a good night's sleep. A good night's sleep helps the heart find its beat and gives the brain a break. Less than clear, the conscience is apt to obsess about tempo and syncopation, worry after where the mind has wandered (likely loitering at an all-night launderette, all agape at the marvels of modern technology, or at a jungle gym, practicing calisthenics).

For best results, clear conscience often, lest a little filth turn into a permanent stain. To address scuffs and smudges, fill a large, lidded jar with four parts water, one part alcohol, two parts galvanized nails. Add soiled conscience and shake well. Repeat as necessary. To dry, lay flat over an open flame.

How to Clean Everything: M

Though meant to last, marriage, unlike most major investments (washing machines, Frigidaires), comes with no warranty or instruction manual. Still, some tried-and-true tricks of the trade may improve maintenance.

Keep clutter to a minimum. Though it is common to hoard every he-said-she-said for posterity, these are rarely reused effectively, waste valuable storage space, and can become, like oily rags in a basement, toxic and highly flammable.

The windows of a marriage must be cleaned regularly— it is a wonder what a clear view can do. Choose window dressings carefully. Blackout blinds and heavy drapery are not recommended. We suggest lace. A high-quality cotton variety will allow sun and moonlight in but maintain a modicum of privacy. Wash in warm, sudsy water, rinse clear, and hang on a taut line to dry. Follow same basic washing instructions for love and anger; line dry love in direct sunlight, anger in a good gale.

Heating systems vary from marriage to marriage; none should be left to run empty. A dry tank can cause permanent damage. Though it may be possible to prime the lines and refuel (at a cost), joins that cannot be replaced may break.

When beyond repair, a broken marriage should be discarded with care: sharp edges and splintered bits boxed, taped, and kept out of reach of pets and small children. Check community calendar for local disposal services.

How to Clean Everything: S

Souls, if not properly maintained, will accumulate grunge: dust, dirty secrets, the daily news. Proper ventilation and regular airing are a must. Sunshine and a little lemon work wonders on pesky dark spots, and, while not a permanent solution, encourage significant fade.

Commercial cleansers are plentiful and readily available, but buyer beware! Their marketing is wholly unregulated. No soul can be returned to its original patina; claims to the contrary are patently false. Though it may be tempting to purchase the latest "miracle cure," a mist of salt water and a good buff are easier on the pocketbook and, if applied regularly, produce an excellent shine.

Note: all souls are permeable and handle water well. Still, care should be taken that no soul be left too long in the damp, as this causes mould. See also: odours (unpleasant), rot, and mildew.

Rachel Carson Writes to Mary Scott Skinker Again, Much Later

I suppose our missing letters do seem
suspicious. This is what happened:
you died, Mary Scott, and your brother
sent my letters back. Each tucked neatly

into its envelope. A brown paper parcel
I slipped under the bed, beside the blue
hat box holding yours. You'd had no time
to prepare; I did. Read each page again and again,

then buried them all in the garden. Warm sun
and earth like crushed velvet. My brother
would've burned them. Our words curling
into flame. Poor Robert, he never did like words

or women. At the hospital, your brother didn't
ask. He and I did not mention your dark hair
pooled like a spill on the cold tile floor, the pale
secretary pressing her ear to your chest, her hand

on your cheek, *Mary, is there someone
we can call?* You whispering my name.
I hadn't seen you since you moved to Dallas.
Two years, Mary Scott, but you knew I would come.

Perhaps your brother was afraid to ask;
pictured garter belts and dildos, the notorious
Bettie Page. Funny, to think of those brother-men
wanting and not wanting to walk in, catch us

side by side playing
pinochle, gin in china cups,
our bodies draped
in cotton nightgowns.

How I did miss those visits, darling,
when you left.

In Which Miss Carson Describes Her Love

I was 22 before I even
saw it, but I always knew.
To love the sea is to envy
the open mouths
of mollusks.
Starfish,
their tender bodies splayed.

Found: *Encyclopedia of Underwater Life*

The characins, catfishes, carps,
and New World knifefishes
are a highly successful group
and display a remarkable mixture
of evolutionary conservatism
and extreme radicalism,
which, when coupled
with the plasticity or variability
at the species level, makes
their taxonomy very difficult.
For such common fish, they
are an enigmatic group.

Over One Million Copies Sold

It would be pleasant to know what a woman
looks like who can write about an exacting
science with such beauty and precision.

—Jonathan Norton Leonard, *New York Times*
book review of *The Sea Around Us*, 1951

No author photo on the jacket of *The Sea*
Around Us, Rachel. Some readers peg you
a man. The rest of us imagine a goddess,

seductive as a pearl oyster. Hair a dark tangle,
the scent of wet salt. Face open as the ocean.
Seashell skin so thin we can almost see

bone. In our dreams you wear a turquoise
dress, gold ribbons. We want you to take it
off. Our hands, the muscles of your thighs

sleek as sharks. When you turn
from us, moonlight unhooks
each sharp silver scale down your spine.

Sea World

Our world has been shaped and modified
by the sea . . . all life everywhere carries
with it the impress of its marine origin.

—Rachel Carson

The great white shark pup hams it up
for underwater cameras; toothy Hollywood grin
to our fear. But is it visions of our bloody
limbs, or a glimpse of ourselves
in the pup's slick fin that alarms us?

Cinderella's stepsisters, we run from mirrors.
Lop off that fin, stick it in soup, a brew to forget
who kills who. We prefer our sharks synthetic, dull,
grey rubber, plopped in the bath. Our Sea World
souvenir.

In Which the Poet Writes Rachel Carson a Fan Letter

Dear Miss Carson,

I've been wondering what you did about your
biological clock. Mine's become a pinball,
banging itself off uterine walls, dull metal thud
to the ovaries. Ricochets up off a rib,

sticks in my heart, ticking. At night it rolls
through my brain, bounces around baby names.
I've read you were named after your grandmother.
When I was small, my grandmother gave me a doll

that looked like a real baby—yellow onesie,
rubbery wrinkles. I called her Rachel. I'd like to say
this was because, even then, I knew you. But I was
a kid who scarfed back Cheez Whiz and Beefaroni

in front of the TV. My doll was named after Nan's
favourite soap star: Rachel on *Another World*.
She was married to Mac. He was a dream.
Funny, isn't it? You and my plastic baby named

Rachel, our grandmothers. I think it's a sign.
Well, gotta go, clock's ticking.

First Lady of the Environment

The lounge for famous people who've made it
to heaven has an open bar, faux-leather sofas,
and a wide-screen TV. Most nights there are fights
over who gets the flicker, arguments about

syndicated reruns, the merits of Technicolor,
but who doesn't love an awards show? Al Gore
gets an Oscar, and the gamblers put money
on Rachel Carson. The next pop culture

comeback, First Lady of the Environment.
She pays it no mind, until Che Guevara
stands before her, takes her hand
in his, nods discreetly towards Pocahontas.

Miss Carson, he says, *if Disney*
makes a movie, you must never watch it.
He is wearing a yellow Che T-shirt.
Pocahontas has taken to haunting

junk shops, rescuing plastic Pocahontas
Barbies. She washes their long hair,
their slim bodies the colour of weak tea.
Knits miniature sweaters and long underwear,
stitches doll-sized patchwork skirts.

She tucks each doll snugly
beneath a buffalo-hide blanket.
Rachel still hears her humming
lullabies at night.

Lending Library, Heaven

Heaven's library held copies of every book that made a ding
'til the tech-wings got wind of e-readers—*My God,
think of the space we'll save!*—modern thinking isn't
really His thing, but real estate was at a premium.

Some rare first editions were dropped back to earth,
appearing in attics and Sally Anns, fun for the auctioneers
and *Antiques Roadshow* fans; the bulk tucked in storage.
Recall notices were sent to all library patrons, which

went well (they'd grown used to letting go), until Hitchcock
sent back *Silent Spring* with pages missing. Horrified,
the head archivist called Jesus Christ, going on and on—
the value of the printed page, respect for public property.
The dead, she wailed, *should know better by now, than the bloody*

living! Back at the office, Jesus finds the flask in his file cabinet.
*Listen, Hitch, the librarians are pitching a fit. What in Pa's name
were you thinking?* Stroking the hat in his lap, Hitchcock slowly
shakes his head. *It's that first chapter. The one where no birds
sing. Christ, I just can't get enough of it.*

Portrait of Rachel Carson
Waiting for David Suzuki

She felt flattered when she learned her book
had changed his life, but it's not as if
he were the first. Many men have
said many things about Miss Carson.

When her BFF finally arrived, Rachel said
she admired his science. They both knew
it was really his face. She'd always
had a hunger for high cheekbones.

Trouble is: he's alive and what is she?
She is a patient woman. Patience
a virtue she has cultivated like
sea mussels. At least it's become easier

to travel. On speaking tours, he meets with
politicians. She waits in coffee shops, tries
to remember the taste of tea. Imagines
the conversations they'll have, what he will

teach her about genetics. She smiles,
thinking of the book critics, the ones
who called her a communist. Spinster.
What would they make of her now?

When he lectures, she likes to sit in the back.
Watch women listen to his voice. She's
heard it all before. Still, sometimes he looks
in her direction and she winks. At night

the hotel sheets lie crisp and bright. When
he falls asleep, she slips in beside. The touch
of her cool hand on the flat of his stomach
does not wake him.

Rachel Carson Comes for Tea

I've spent the morning tidying and baking.
I've swept and re-swept the floor. The house
is a party. How many first stars, pennies in wells
for this visit? And now, you at the door

in a blue summer raglan. *Miss Carson, please,*
come in. You smile, *Call me Rachel.* Compliment
the tea biscuits I've baked us, the Bauline Line blueberry
jam. The top of my vintage table (modern when you were

alive) is Arborite, lipstick red. Your hands are so pale it's
hard not to touch them. I want to say you're a rebel and
a lady and your life has made mine better. I want to say
I love the photo of you in a ball cap and short-shorts, shin-

deep in sea. I want to say you have beautiful
legs. But this switch from the longed-for has thrown me
like a sculpin from saltwater—*Miss Carson, more tea?*

Legacy / Challenge

When Rachel applied for a visitor's pass
to appear on Earth, she planned to observe
environmentalists, attend meetings, sit on
boards. She'd write a final report focussed

on progress. The committee said this was
fine, if she agreed to certain conditions.
There'd be no scooting back to the cottage
in Maine, chatting up wardens at the R.

Carson Wildlife Refuge. She must steer
clear of the Northeastern seaboard.
Rachel argued this was unnecessary, overkill,
she'd borrow sunglasses from Jackie O,

No one will recognize me. The chairman
said this might be so, but after all the Elvis
incidents, they weren't taking any chances.
She must also agree to avoid Suzuki and Gore.

Rachel sighed, *Fine. Where do you suggest
I go?* The committee recommended Canada.
In Ottawa, she joined the Green Party, attended
rallies, called constituents. The hang-ups began

to bring her down. Elizabeth May said she looked
familiar. Time to move on. In Toronto, she joined
the WWF, Sierra Club, Environmental Defence,
but after a while they all looked the same: petitions

and publicity campaigns, fleece and hiking boots, keys
on carabiners. How to keep track of who was saving which
flagship species? On the ferry to Argentia she talked cod
with a drunk trucker. He used to fish, but there'd been

a collapse, a moratorium. *The cod, missus,*
is gone. She ordered a double rye and ginger.
Scheduled to attend a public forum on the lack of
sewage treatment in St. John's harbour, she misread

the date, arrived at the church hall just in time for
bingo. Which is where you'll find her every
Tuesday night—twelve cards and a tin of Lime Crush,
sitting with the women from the ladies dart league.

An Intern Catches up on Admin

Please let me know in a hurry who Rachel Carson is.
That girl keeps me awake night after night.

—Reader letter to the New Yorker, 1954

May 27, 2007

Dear Sir,

Thank you for your letter re: Rachel Carson.
We apologize for the delay in our response.
Unfortunately, no one on staff has ever met
the woman; all correspondence carried out

via an agent. We did find one photo: blurry
(facsimile enclosed). Pity her face
is obscured by the desk lamp, or perhaps it's a
stack of books. We have it on good authority

that beneath that desk she is wearing
fishnet stockings. Patent leather pumps.
At night she sleeps in a claw-foot tub, slim legs
turning to tail. You'll never touch

a creature such as this,
but lean close, ask nice
and she might talk dirty:
heptachlor, dieldrin, DDT.

Notes

The poems in the second section of this manuscript, "Spinster," have been written in response to the life and work of Rachel Carson. While they are works of fiction, they take factual information into account. Rachel Carson, an American writer and scientist, was the author of *Silent Spring*, a book many consider the catalyst of the modern environmental movement. *Silent Spring* raises concerns about the long-term effects of indiscriminate pesticide use, and takes an ecological approach to the way we live in the world. Published in 1962, *Silent Spring* received a great deal of media attention, in part because of a smear campaign launched by the pesticide industry, which did not take kindly to Carson's critiques. Pesticide use was widespread at the time, including in a domestic context. Carson was called hysterical, a communist, her scientific credibility was questioned, and much was made of the fact that she was middle-aged and unmarried. In addition to *Silent Spring*, Rachel Carson wrote three best-selling books about the ocean. In 1954, her book *The Edge of the Sea* was serialized in the *New Yorker*.

Silent Spring has never gone out of print; Al Gore (former vice president of the United States) and David Suzuki (geneticist, television presenter, and environmental activist) have said reading the book inspired them to become environmentalists. The subsequent banning of DDT, among other pesticides, is directly related to Rachel Carson and *Silent Spring*. Unfortunately, Carson did not live to see the full impact of her work. She died of breast cancer in 1964; she was 56.

The following texts have been important to my research on Rachel Carson: "'Silence, Miss Carson!': Science, Gender, and the Reception of *Silent Spring*" by Michael B. Smith; *Rachel Carson: Witness for Nature* by Linda Lear; *The House of Life: Rachel Carson at Work* by Paul Brooks; *Always, Rachel: The Letters of Rachel Carson and Dorothy Freeman, 1952-1964* edited by Martha Freeman; *Rachel Carson: Legacy and Challenge* edited by Lisa H. Sideris and Kathleen Dean Moore; and *The Recurring Silent Spring* by H. Patricia Hynes.

The epigraph to this book and the poem "The Chrome Chair," is a quote, possibly misremembered, from the Newfoundland and Labrador Historical Society Symposium, 2003: The Idea of Newfoundland: Nationalism, Identity & Culture from the 19th Century to Present. Memorial University English professor Shane O'Dea gave a talk at that symposium titled "Culture and Country: The Role of Arts and Heritage in the Revival of Nationalism," and while I no longer have my notes from the symposium, the sentiment conveyed regarding confederation and chrome chairs is echoed in O'Dea's essay "Culture and Country: The Role of the Arts and Heritage in the Nationalist Revival in Newfoundland," in the *Journal of Newfoundland Studies* 19 (2) 2003.

The definition of splinter is cherry-picked from the *Oxford English Dictionary (OED)* online and is not the complete dictionary entry; the definition of spinster is also cherry-picked from the *OED* online, with some poetic embellishments in italics.

The title of the poem "They Loved These Things Too" and all italicized phrases are taken directly from a poem with the same title by Lisa Jarnot.

The epigraph to "Feminists in Heaven" can be found, with quite a bit of text between the question and answer, "In The Matter of A

Reference As To The Meaning of The Word 'Persons'" in Section 24 of the *British North America Act*, 1867, April 24, 1928, SCR 276. Supreme Court Judgements transcript, Supreme Court of Canada website. The poem references Emily Murphy, who initiated Canada's "Persons" Case. Murphy, along with four others—Henrietta Muir Edwards, Nellie McClung, Louise McKinney and Irene Parlby—petitioned the Canadian government to allow women to be appointed to the Senate of Canada as "qualified persons." In reference to this case, these five women are commonly referred to as the Famous Five.

The "How to Clean Everything" poems take their titles from the book *How to Clean Everything* by Alma Chestnut Moore, first published in 1952. My own copy (third edition; revised and updated; over 400,000 copies sold) was published in 1977; I found it in a library book sale in Southport, Maine, where Rachel Carson had a cottage.

The lines in the cento "Found: *Encyclopedia of Underwater Life*" are taken from the entry for "Characins, Catfishes, Carps, and Allies" in *Encyclopedia of Underwater Life*, edited by Andrew Campbell and John Dawes.

Earlier versions of some poems in this book have previously appeared in *Arc Poetry Magazine*, *The Best Canadian Poetry in English*, 2011, the *Fiddlehead*, the *Newfoundland Quarterly* and *Riddle Fence*.

Acknowledgements

To the kickass team of women at *Riddle Fence*: Megan Gail Coles, Elisabeth de Mariaffi and Carmella Gray-Cosgrove. Thank you for your brilliance, patience and for having the audacity to start a publishing imprint in the year 2023.

To my amazing editor Sandra Ridley—thank you for editing this manuscript with such precision, care, and enthusiasm. I could never have turned this pile of poems into a real, live book without you. Thanks also to copy editor extraordinaire Allison LaSorda for the final sweep and polish.

Thank you to photographer Stacey Croucher for the perfect cover image and to graphic designer Graham Blair for putting it all together so beautifully.

Thank you to John Devereaux (aka my best brother) and Duncan Major of Perfect Day for the author's photo; I appreciate your efforts to make me look presentable.

To my friend and mentor Mary Dalton. I started writing Rachel Carson poems in a creative writing course Mary taught at Memorial University. Thank you for that catalyst, for the inspiration your own poetry provides, and for everything you do to foster and promote poetry in this place.

The poem "Playthings" was originally written for the 2005 CBC Radio Poetry Face-Off. The late Stan Dragland edited an early version of the poem out of the kindness of his heart; I sure do wish he and his kind heart were still here.

A handful of these poems were previously published in the chapbook *Cardiogram* (Baseline Press, 2011). Thank you to Karen

Schindler, publisher, for inviting me to be part of that inaugural run of Baseline Press's lovely little books.

The poem "Quelle Affaire" was made into a short film with the same title by filmmaker Ruth Lawrence. The film is saucy and super pretty and it was so much fun to be part of it all. Thank you to Ruth for that opportunity.

Different iterations of this manuscript benefited from time spent at the Banff Writing Studio (2007 and 2009) and the Banff Wired Writing Studio (2014), many thanks to the programs' poetry mentors for their advice and insight, and to everyone involved (mentors and mentees) for the friendships and fun.

Grants from the Newfoundland and Labrador Arts Council have helped me at various stages of writing; I appreciate that support.

To my parents, Bernice and Jack Devereaux, who have always been a shining light in my life. Thank you for your giant generous hearts and your unending support for all my endeavors, poetic and otherwise. And to my Aunt Carol, my other mother, you had such a talent for celebrating life; I wish you and your gorgeous smile were here to celebrate with us now.

Finally, to Chris Hogan and our beauties, Seamus and Rose—you'll always have my heart.

Danielle Devereaux grew up in St. John's, Newfoundland where she lives now with her partner, their two children and two cats. Her poetry has appeared in *Riddle Fence, Arc Poetry Magazine, The Fiddlehead, Newfoundland Quarterly,* and *The Best Canadian Poetry in English 2011.* Her chapbook, *Cardiogram,* was published in 2011 by Baseline Press. "Quelle Affaire," a poem from the chapbook, was made into a short film by director Ruth Lawrence. An earlier draft of *The Chrome Chair* was shortlisted for the NLCU Fresh Fish Award for Emerging Writers. Danielle is an alumnus of the Banff Centre for the Arts Writing Studio, holds a Bachelor of Arts and a Master of Women's Studies from Memorial University, and has done doctoral work in Communications Studies at Concordia University. She has worked as a freelance writer and editor, and currently works in communications at Memorial University's School of Social Work.